AIR
GUITAR

AIR GUITAR

BRUNO MACDONALD

A User's Guide

WHAT EVERY AXEMAN NEEDS to KNOW

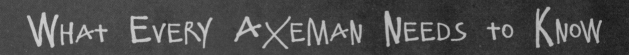

INSIGHT EDITIONS

San Rafael, California

INSIGHT
EDITIONS

PO Box 3088
San Rafael, CA 94912
www.insighteditions.com

Library of Congress Cataloging-in-Publication Data available.

ISBN: 978-1-60887-071-4

Copyright © 2012 Elephant Book Company Limited
35 Fournier Street
London E1 6QE
www.elephantbookcompany.com

Illustrations copyright © 2012 Elephant Book Company Limited

Editorial Director: Will Steeds
Project Editor: Laura Ward
Cover and interior design: Lindsey Johns
Copyeditor: Kristi Hein
Illustrator: Rob Brandt
Color Reproduction: Modern Age Repro House Ltd., Hong Kong

Manufactured in China

First Edition

10 9 8 7 6 5 4 3 2 1

CONTENTS

GETTING STARTED   7

AIR GUITAR MOVES   19

All the air guitar moves you'll ever need, from the demanding duck walk to the performance-enhancing power slide—all usefully labeled learner (★), amateur (★★), or master axeman (★★★)

GOING PRO   53

Fifty air guitar anthems you've gotta try, from the Beatles to Bullet for My Valentine

Plus ten tunes you should never, EVER try . . .

AIR GUITAR: FROM THE NECK DOWN

Freddie Mercury did it. Hormone-addled adolescents do it. Grown men do it in the privacy of their own homes (and, sometimes, in dark public gatherings). There are even specialist computer games that *encourage* you to do it.

It is air guitar. Like sex, drugs, and Keith Richards, it is one of the staples of rock 'n' roll.

Yet—unlike sex, drugs, and Keith Richards—it can be safely attempted by any amateur enthusiast. You don't need to know a thing about notes and chords. You don't need an army of roadies. You don't even need to invest in *Guitar Hero* or *Rock Band*. All you need is confidence and a copy of this book.

Naysayers may argue that air guitar is a sad, solitary activity that shouldn't be encouraged. But the same is truer of blogging—which has to be the most masturbatory activity of our age.

Air guitar, in contrast, expresses neither inner torment nor suppressed sexual fetishes. It expresses our enthusiasm for the music that moves us, and our deep-rooted need to *rock*.

AIRY ASSES

Billy Joel noted, after his groundbreaking shows in Russia during the Cold War: "One of the guys in our production company went over to the Soviet Union and [filmed] a heavy metal concert and there was this kid playing air guitar just like they do in Toledo, Ohio, and my heart went out to this kid . . . I've seen that kid in Omaha, Nebraska, I've seen him in Tallahassee, Florida, and I've seen him in Lexington, Kentucky. It's the same kid. He's making an ass of himself playing the air guitar. So how different can we be?"

And it's not just party-hearty members of the paying public who raise the imaginary axe. Buddy Guy recalled his friend Stevie Ray Vaughan: "I remember standing with him on the side of the stage while Eric [Clapton] was playing. He was

sort of playing air guitar, fingering along with what Eric played. After he died, man, for some reason, I kept thinking of that: him standing there playing phantom notes."

Fans of Zeppelin, Queen, and the Who will recall Plant, Mercury, and Daltrey, respectively, holding their microphone leads in a way suggesting nothing less than Guitar Envy. Even Britney Spears strummed the air toward the end of her video for "Do Somethin'"— which may explain the similarity between that song and Muse's subsequent "Supermassive Black Hole."

Air guitar can form the first steps that a rock 'n' roller takes on the stairway to stardom. "I used to play air drums, air guitar, air singing, everything, in the dark with the music playing really loud," admitted Debbi Peterson of the Bangles. (Unsurprisingly, that wasn't enough for Van Halen front man David Lee Roth: "Some people play air guitar or sing along with the radio. Well, I took it twelve steps further.")

More typically, however, air guitar is an ideal medium that fans can use to connect on a satisfyingly physical level with the music they love.

It's ageless, it's universal, and it's all in this book. Rock on, friends.

GETTING STARTED

BASIC DOS AND DON'ts

As Boy Scouts and festival-goers know, it's best to be prepared. Unlike Boy Scouts or festival-goers, air guitarists don't need Swiss Army knives or disposable toilet seat covers. However, if you're going to take the art of air guitar seriously—and not just strum along absentmindedly when Green Day comes on the radio—you need to do your homework. Get the mindset, study hard, ignore anyone who questions whether this is appropriate behavior . . . and, in the wise words of Def Leppard, "Rock rock ('til you drop)." You may never scale the heights of *American Idol* winners, but you're less likely to become an object of national ridicule or record a second album that sells forty-seven copies. And never lose heart. Even Slash admitted that, in his preplaying days, "I had no idea which instrument made each sound . . . I knew what a guitar was, but I had no idea of the differences between a guitar and a bass."

▶ DO

Lock 'n' roll

In the *Risky Business* scene that immortalized air guitar on the silver screen, Tom Cruise slides across the floor in his socks to Bob Seger's "Old Time Rock and Roll." We're not recommending TC as a role model, but he got one thing right: waiting until he had the house to himself and locking the doors before stripping to his underwear and grabbing an imaginary axe.

▶ DON'T

Shoegaze

Rock is littered with fine musicians whose act consisted of peering intently at their frets and/or feet. However, none but the nerdiest would want to *be* Kevin Shields of My Bloody Valentine or Mike Rutherford of Genesis. This is why God invented light shows (and, in Shields' case, brain-melting volume—equally tricky to simulate with thin air).

▶ DO

Lubricate
(relax—we mean Dutch courage)

"Join me for a drink, boys / We're gonna make a big noise," is AC/DC's sage-like message. Far be it from us to recommend alcohol's inhibition-loosening powers, but unless you find Perrier bubbles intoxicating, Jack Daniels may be the way to go. (Take it easy: As Ozzy sings, "Wine is fine but whiskey's quicker / Suicide is slow with liquor.")

▶ DON'T

Put the YOU in YouTube

If you post footage of yourself air guitaring on the Internet, you might elicit encouraging comments like "Nice technique, dude. Way to go." You are more likely, however, to receive offensive and badly spelled criticism. This may help to harden your resolve, but it's likely to also involve you in a time-wasting slanging match with a twelve-year-old troll in a time zone light years away (or as good as) and in a language resembling none you know.

9

▶ DO

Warm-up

Air guitar is like any other form of exercise (except it's not necessary to wear shorts or take communal showers afterward). If you give yourself a vigorous workout without first stretching your neck, arms, legs, and back, you will wake up the next day excruciatingly sore and unable to impersonate any guitarist other than Mick Mars of Mötley Crüe.

▶ DON't

Confuse computer games with the real thing

It could be argued that *Guitar Hero* and *Rock Band* have legitimized air guitar. But it could also be argued that these games have: (1) reduced a noble art to the level of *Frogger* and (2) corrupted the spirit of air guitar from a physical embodiment of our love for music into a brow-furrowing, point-scoring exercise. Play if you must, but approach with caution.

▶ DO

Keep your eyes open

Many a "real" guitarist signals a rapturous response to his own playing by squeezing his eyes shut—in fact, B.B. King has made a career out of it. Air guitarists, however, should avoid this: If you're at home, you'll regret it if someone walks in on you; onstage, you will elicit mockery rather than pity if you fall over.

▶ DON'T

Fall off the stage

There's a reason why falling off the stage is associated with singers, such as Scott Weiland, Patti Smith, and Steven Tyler—guitarists are just too cool to do it. And, by all accounts, it hurts. Furthermore, while we're on the subject: Don't air guitar in the shower. You'll slip and fall. And if someone catches you at it, good luck explaining that you were *only* air guitaring.

▶ **DO**

Confess to your partner

Air guitaring is, to us, as natural as breathing and burping. You don't think about it, you just do it. You can therefore drift off into a reverie of fantasy fretboarding, only to abruptly realize that your better half is staring at you, amused or aghast. But stand up for your right to rock—and, who knows, maybe he or she will join you for a K.K./Tipton routine.

AIR ANTHEMS...

You can also use your prep time to warm up your ears. Some suggested air anthems for the preplaying period:

★ *"Are You Ready"*
by Thin Lizzy (*Live and Dangerous*, 1978)

★ *"Gettin' Ready"*
by UFO (*Lights Out*, 1977)

★ *"Ready to Rock"*
by the Michael Schenker Group (*MSG*, 1981) . . .

You get the idea.

▶ **DON'T**

Wear jewelry

Yes, Slash wears bangles and bracelets. Yes, Keef wears that big skull. Yes, Lemmy is a walking advertisement for the London jewelry store The Great Frog. But note the common factor: Hudson, Richards, and Kilmister are three of the coolest people to have walked the Earth, whereas you are an air guitarist who has raided his mom's jewelry box.

▶ DO

Practice

Did Eddie Van Halen wake up one morning able to leap gymnastically from one note to another? No, he did not. Did Jimi Hendrix wake up one morning and inadvertently rewrite the rules of rock? No, he did not. Will you simply wake up one morning and be the world's most spectacular air guitarist? No, you will not. Practice!

▶ DON'T

Be intimidated by real guitarists

When you learn to drive, impatient idiots behind you will happily forget that a license did not just materialize in their wallet. They, too, had to start somewhere—but this does not stop them honking their horn, gesturing, and dangerously tailgating. You will no doubt encounter similar stupidity as an air guitarist.

Console yourself with the thought that these morons take themselves far too seriously and that you, in contrast, actually enjoy life.

13

ACCESSORIES

All Bob Dylan—and, in due course, Jimi Hendrix and U2—needed in "All Along the Watchtower" was "a red guitar, three chords, and the truth." For air guitarists, an even more economical allowance will do the trick: hands (in a pinch, one hand will do), music (onstage, on a stereo, or simply in your head), and either privacy or an indulgent audience.

That said, there are accoutrements that can elevate a humble air guitar session.

White's all right

Black is back

DRESSED TO KILL

Many an axe hero has flaunted the basic rock 'n' roll dress code, from the plaid shirts of Kurt Cobain to the billowing sleeves of Jimmy Page, and from the bare chest of Ted Nugent to the aluminum foil shoulder pads of Ace Frehley. But to allow maximum movement and to connote authenticity in spades, the humble T-shirt cannot be beaten.

Acceptable variants include plain white (see Springsteen and the Ramones) or plain black (see Metallica and, contrarily, the Ramones). Yellow or any similarly cheerful color will make you look like a member of Loverboy and should therefore be avoided.

Torn T-shirts are acceptable—they didn't do the Sex Pistols any harm—and are certainly preferable to a suspiciously pristine *Appetite for Destruction* number that might as well still have the big box store price tag hanging off of it.

Rip's rip

Band logos are fine, though steer clear of Motörhead, the Ramones, and the Misfits—in other words, any act better known for their T's than their tunes.

Glittery Iron Maiden and Kiss logos or Stones tongues will make it obvious that you have raided your sister's wardrobe for shirts that were inexplicably fashionable about a decade ago. Led Zeppelin are also off limits, unless you were actually *at* one of the seventies concerts that so many of their T-shirts seem to celebrate.

"Witty" slogans should be approached with caution. Sebastian Bach's "AIDS kills fags dead" T had the unintended, albeit appropriate, effect of killing his career dead, while Keith Richards' "Who the fuck is Mick Jagger?" only worked because he is Keef, who can officially do anything.

Finally, cap sleeves are for girls.

Yell oh no

Big girl

WHAT A RACKET

Links are legion between tennis and rock 'n' roll. Lars Ulrich was set to follow in his father's professional footsteps to the clay court before a severe attack of NWoBHM (New Wave of British Heavy Metal) led him to cofound Metallica. Gavin Rossdale is buddies with Roger Federer, and on the court he has made sporting—albeit not very chivalrous—mincemeat of Lindsay Davenport and Chris Evert (if only Rossdale had stuck to tennis and not inflicted Bush on us). Robert Plant once expressed a wish to "be the best tennis player on my block and sing with the gods." Legendary tour promoter Larry Magid remarked, of the likes of Stefan Edberg, "These players have achieved rock-star status." Adam Duritz of Counting Crows admitted to being "five years old doing 'Can't Buy Me Love' in front of the mirror with a tennis racket."

Most tellingly, John McEnroe and Pat Cash enlisted Roger Daltrey and Iron Maiden's Steve Harris and Nicko McBrain (billed, appallingly, as the Full Metal Rackets) for a 1991 charity single assault on Zeppelin's "Rock and Roll."

But the best-known link between tennis and rock is the racket—whose shape, dimensions, and availability have made it the air guitarist's weapon of choice since time immemorial. Adding to their all-around greatness, rackets have actual strings—albeit ones so tough and tightly wound they'll inflict minor injury if overly ambitiously played.

Avoid squash and badminton rackets—unless, perhaps, you are pretending to be Steve Howe leaping nimbly through the convoluted time signatures of an early Yes classic. Racquetball variants are completely unacceptable.

Racket

Geetar

15

DUST YOUR BROOM

Envelope-pushing air guitarists can adapt a variety of implements to their needs. The author of this book was once caught—by bemused builders—miming to Editors' "The Racing Rats" with a rake that he was supposed to be using to clean out a stable.

Brooms, on the other hand, have two advantages. The weight at one end makes a broom a lot more satisfactory than flimsier racket substitutes, such as rulers. And, assuming you can locate the traditional "witch's broom" rather than a common push broom, it can look—OK, only if you squint—like a Gibson Flying V. For evidence, fast-forward the 1993 movie *Mrs. Doubtfire* to an iconic scene in which Robin Williams air guitars with this household-cleaning favorite to Aerosmith's "Dude (Looks Like a Lady)."

Push broom:

No

Witch's broom:

Yes

Avoid mops. Although the mop head can add weight and flamboyance, they tend to be wet and/or smelly.

16

FRIENDS WILL BE FRIENDS

Misinformed public opinion may hold that air guitar is usually practiced in solitary conditions. But nothing beats a more communal vibe, be it a stadium full of AC/DC fans, rock clubbers going nuts to "Killing in the Name," or two or three buddies in a bedroom.

An associate or two opens up a whole new vista of opportunity, whether it's the Mick 'n' Keef/Tyler and Perry–style sharing of an imaginary mic, or the syncopated axe-swinging that runs in the veins of rock 'n' roll from the Shadows to Status Quo (see the climax of any live version of Kiss's "Deuce" for a particularly iconic routine).

ALTOGETHER NOW

MONEY: IT'S A GAS

Coins make exemplary makeshift plectrums—just ask Brian May, who has always preferred the former to the latter, and who has effectively transformed money into lots and lots and lots more money. A discussion of this very topic on guitarzone.com rated British 20-pence and 50-pence pieces as particularly good for tapping, but you may wish to use less valuable coins, as they will inevitably slip from your excitedly sweaty fingers, to roll under beds, couches, cats, and so on.

PAPERS

Other substitute plectrums suggested on guitarzone include train tickets, cigarette-paper packets, paper clips, credit cards, and bits of plastic hacked from ice-cream cartons and CDs. We, however, take no responsibility if you use any of the more insanely dangerous items from this list.

THUNDER AND LIGHTNING

Judicious use of household items can turn any air guitar session into an arena-worthy sensation. What is Pink Floyd's light show but a couple of flashlights and laser pointers in a dark room? What are amp stacks but a few piled-up boxes? What is dry ice but carbon dioxide? (Although, to be honest, there's a bit more to dry ice than that. And don't even think about messing with liquid nitrogen.)

Carefully placed props can be explained away to suspicious partners as evidence of rigorous spring-cleaning or the beginnings of an art installation project that will make you rich and famous. Both of these will, in due course, benefit your other half, so they can have no cause for complaint.

MAKIN' FACES

"The concept of 'the rock guitar solo' in the eighties," complained Frank Zappa, "has pretty much been reduced to: 'Weedly weedly wee, make a face, hold your guitar like it's your weenie, point it heavenward, and look like you're really doing something. Then you get a big ovation while the smoke bombs go off, and the motorized lights in your truss twirl around.'"

The old curmudgeon may have had a point, but don't forget that Frank made albums like *Shut Up 'n Play Yer Guitar* consisting of nothing but solos, and that he gave weedly wee–meister Steve Vai his first big break. So let's accentuate the positives of the "make a face" clause. It communicates a variety of emotions, from "I am the living embodiment of the devil's music" to "I am astonished at the notes coming from my own instrument." It gives your audience something to look at if you don't have pyrotechnics. And, crucially for air guitarists, it distracts people from the fact that you're making entirely the wrong chord shapes.

★ Air Anthem:

"Love in an Elevator"
Aerosmith
Pump, 1989

WEEDLY WEEDLY WEE

LEVEL: ★★★
Amateur Axeman

Try these popular variants:

DEMONIC

As a popular office motto has it, You Don't Have to Be Gene Simmons to Work Here . . . But It Helps! For proof that this can be distinctive even without truckloads of makeup, check out Kiss's *Lick It Up* cover.

HAPPY

Most famously associated with Eddie Van Halen. For years, it seemed he was enjoying his playing as much as we were. Then he kept firing band members and we found out what a grumpy bugger he really was.

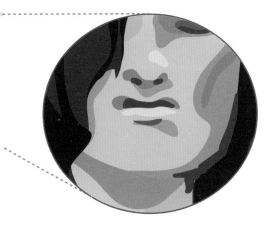

POUTING

While lesser mortals opt for routine orgasm expressions, Jimmy Page expresses satisfaction by sucking in his cheeks and puckering his lips. Drawback: Audiences may think you're channeling Mick Jagger by mistake.

Steer clear of Furrowed Brow Frowning as practiced by Kirk Hammett and Dave Gilmour (not very interesting), Crazed Gurning as practiced by Ted Nugent (works only if you're wearing a loincloth), and Eyes Closed in Rapture as practiced by B.B. King (see Dos and Don'ts; also, too easily mistaken for Stevie Wonder).

DEVIL HORNS

"The first time I saw it was when Gene Simmons did it onstage," recalled Mötley Crüe's Nikki Sixx. The Kiss figurehead does indeed take credit for rock's most ubiquitous hand gesture (after the middle finger)—although, as Ronnie James Dio quipped, "Gene Simmons will tell you that he invented it, but, then again, Gene invented breathing, and shoes, and everything . . . "

Dio was, in fact, the man who brought the "maloik" (*il malocchio*) to the masses. He learned it from his superstitious Italian grandmother—who would raise her index and little finger to ward off anyone giving her "the evil eye"—and deployed it as a visual trademark like the "V" peace signs of Ozzy Osbourne, whom Dio succeeded as front man of Black Sabbath. "Invented? No," Dio admitted in the 2005 rockumentary *Metal: A Headbanger's Journey*. "But perfected, and made it important? Yes, because I did it so much. Especially within the confines of that great band, Sabbath, which had this incredible name already."

★ Air Anthem:

"Gypsy"

Dio
Holy Diver, 1983

LEVEL:

Learner

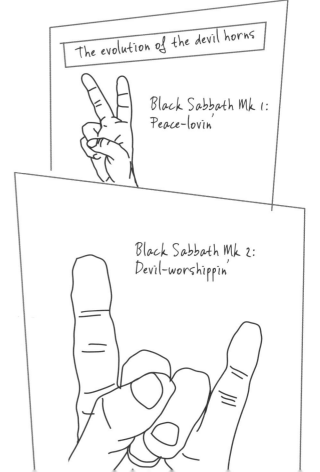

The evolution of the devil horns

Black Sabbath Mk 1:
Peace-lovin'

Black Sabbath Mk 2:
Devil-worshippin'

GRR...

FEELIN' HORNY

Initially, the horns remained largely confined to the metal community. "I've never done it to an audience and meant it," protested Def Leppard's Joe Elliott. "That's Dungeons & Dragons territory." These days—thanks largely to the rock chic that sees people wearing T-shirts for bands they'd never listen to—the sign of the horns is as common at shows as camera phones and warm beer. Some rockers use it even outside the arena. "It's like breathing," admitted Judas Priest's metal god Rob Halford. "I'll probably throw the devil sign at the guys in my coffee shop."

Although using the horns while you're playing is a wee bit impractical (unless you want to demonstrate an innovative fret technique), it's useful to insert into any gaps. It will establish solidarity between you and your audience and look less "Judd Nelson at the end of *The Breakfast Club*" than an air-punch.

And, handily, it's similar to the sign language for "I love you," so you might just get a date with a nearby hard-of-hearing person.

23

SMASH!

Anyone dedicated enough to read this book cover to cover will discover the words "Pete" and "Townshend" cropping up with remarkable regularity—and it is to Uncle Pete that we must again turn as we turn the spotlight onto smashing guitars.

★ Air Anthem:
"Black Diamond"
Kiss
Alive!, 1975

"It happened by complete accident," he told *Rolling Stone*. "I was playing the guitar and it hit the ceiling. It broke, and it kind of shocked me, 'cause I didn't particularly want it to go." Dismayed by the audience's apathetic reaction to this personal tragedy, Townshend decided to finish the job—and, in doing so, created an iconic effect. Aspiring stars duly aped it; Deep Purple, for example, were thrown off a support slot on a Cream tour when Ritchie Blackmore's destructive antics threatened to upstage the headliners.

In the seventies, Paul Stanley turned the breaking of an imitation guitar into a ritual intrinsic to the Kiss spectacle. Meanwhile, the Clash's *London Calling* sleeve immortalized the last moments in the life of one of Paul Simonon's basses. (In a less celebrated instance, Joe Strummer was arrested in Hamburg in 1980 for smashing a guitar over a fan.)

NEVER MIND THE MONEY

By the eighties, guitars were too expensive for anyone to demolish, but the nineties saw a revival thanks to Nirvana. Kurt Cobain initially smashed one to express annoyance with drummer Chad Channing, only to find that audiences went nuts for these well-worn theatrics. "I don't do it nearly as much as everyone thinks I do," Cobain protested. "I just wait for a good time to do it . . . like when I'm pissed off, or if I want to show off in front of Courtney. Or if I'm appearing on TV . . . I have my guitar-smashing room in the back, where I practice four hours a day." Nirvana even immortalized the act in "Endless Nameless," the *Nevermind* cut that sprang from an abortive attempt at "Lithium."

LEVEL:
★
Learner

"SEE ME, FEEL ME" AND STAND BACK . . .

Air guitar smashing can provide an eye-catching climax to your performance, and it has significant advantages over the real thing: It costs you nothing, and there's no chance of a stray splinter or string rendering you blind. Just remember not to choose a song with a fade-out: This will make you look very foolish indeed.

LEGS AKIMBO

Although they only ever fight photographers and are the most pampered people on the planet, rock stars claim to have, as Bon Scott memorably sang, "the biggest balls of them all."

Irrespective of whether they're sufficiently blessed to warrant it, rock stars are required to stand with legs spread. It spells sex, it spells insouciance, it spells rock, and you must do it if you don't wish to be mistaken for an early sixties beat guitarist or a prissy indie wimp.

★ Air Anthem:

"Durango '95"

The Ramones
We're Outta Here!, 1997

LEVEL:

Learner

26

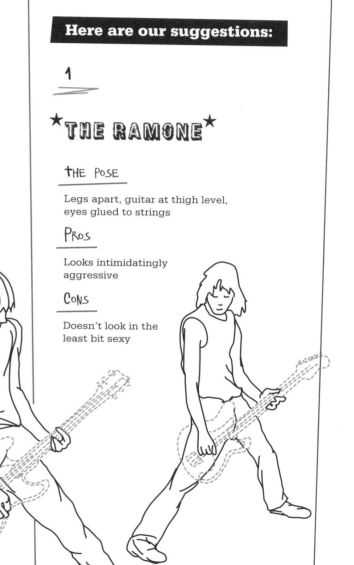

Here are our suggestions:

1

THE RAMONE

THE POSE

Legs apart, guitar at thigh level, eyes glued to strings

PROS

Looks intimidatingly aggressive

CONS

Doesn't look in the least bit sexy

★ Air Anthem:

"Caroline"

Status Quo
Live at the N.E.C., 1984

2

★ THE QUO ★

THE POSE

Legs apart at sensible angle,
guitar at crotch level

PROS

Ideal for moving your hips in time
to a twelve-bar boogie

CONS

Inappropriate for anything more
complex than Status Quo or Kiss

LEVEL:

Learner

3

★ THE PAGEY ★

THE POSE

Weight on one leg, other leg outstretched, back arched, head up (think of a cat, stretching in self-congratulatory satisfaction), guitar raised so its neck is parallel with your body

PROS

Adds emphasis to a particularly weedly-weeing solo

CONS

You may fall over; inappropriate for anything less complex than Led Zeppelin

★ Air Anthem:
"Achilles' Last Stand"

Led Zeppelin
Presence, 1976

LEVEL: ★★
Amateur Axeman

LEVEL: ★★
Amateur Axeman

★ Air Anthem:

"The Wild One"

Suzi Quatro
Quatro, 1974

4

★ THE QUATRO ★
(for the gals)

THE POSE

Legs saucily apart, bottom backwards, chest to the fore

PROS

Looks fierce (even John Sykes and Steve Harris, despite their lack of cleavage, often lean over their instruments)

CONS

Can look like you're constipated; only the drummer benefits from your derriere unless you spin around to wiggle it (inadvisable unless you're Justin Hawkins or you are actually female)

5

★ THE HOOKY ★

THE POSE

Legs almost in splits position, guitar mere inches from the ground

PROS

Looks astonishingly athletic

CONS

Uncomfortable; medically inadvisable; looks faintly ridiculous unless your audience realizes that you're pretending to be Peter Hook

★ Air Anthem:

"Dead Souls"

Joy Division
Still, 1981

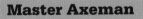

LEVEL:
Master Axeman

★KNEELIN' AND A-ROCKIN'★

Any doubts about the significance of kneeling in rock 'n' roll can be swiftly banished by a glance at the cover of Thin Lizzy's *Live and Dangerous*. There's Phil Lynott, fist clenched, guitar raised to the heavens, and Spandex stretched to breaking point over the cucumber stuffed in his underpants.

Lyrical references to this activity usually involve lovelorn types rendered weak-kneed by love—or, if you're Kiss, young ladies inexplicably eager to please tubby New Yorkers in makeup. As an onstage activity, however, it usually signifies a guitarist whose amazing flurries of notes have literally knocked him off his feet. Think of Eddie Van Halen, one leg tucked under his behind, the other stretched out, guitar neck pointing in phallic fashion to the lighting rig—and, all the while, Eddie's mouth agape in delight at his own whizzkiddery. (To be fair, the rest of the world was just as amazed and delighted as he was.)

★ Air Anthem:

"Warriors"

Thin Lizzy
Live and Dangerous, 1978

LEVEL: ★ ★
Amateur Axeman

30

Goodness, I certainly am rather splendid.

RISE AND FALL

Others have put their own unique twist on bending legs. The Shadows used it in their choreographic arsenal. ("We'd wander about the stage," recalled Hank Marvin. "Lie on our backs, shake our legs in the air, kneel on the floor—all kinds of wild, abandoned rock 'n' roll movements.") Hendrix would lay his guitar on the stage and kneel beside it, the better to aim lighter fuel onto it. David Bowie knelt before Mick Ronson in a then-shocking tableau of fellatio (not a move you should imitate in an air guitar situation, even if you hoodwink a pal into helping you out). The reliably entertaining Scorpions would kneel down, then collapse onto their backs.

Kneeling is, therefore, a useful dramatic device. But beware of the pitfalls. For a start, it could mean that only the front row can see you. You may split a treasured pair of pants. It will probably hasten the onset of arthritis. And if you can't get up without falling over, you won't be able to hear your music over the sound of people laughing.

Note that loud music will obscure tiresome creaking in joints

THE WINDMILL

"Bowling" was Pete Townshend's tongue-in-cheek explanation for how he learned his trademark stage move. The more prosaic truth is that he had observed Keith Richards warming up by raising his hand above his head, then bringing it down across his guitar. (Townshend later confessed this to the Stones legend; Keef, he reported, "looked at me like I was a germ.") In the hands of the Who guitarist, this simple gesture became iconic: witness Billy Duffy windmilling a Gibson on the cover of the Cult's 1989 rocktacular *Sonic Temple*.

The downsides—and here's where air guitar really has an advantage over the real thing—include losing fingernails, breaking strings, and playing wrong chords. Townshend himself threatened to retire the move when the Who returned to the road in 1989. "When I windmill, I break off the ends of my fingers . . ." he told *Rolling Stone*. "And I can't do that to myself. I don't care enough about the audience and I don't care enough about the music. I care more about the state of my fingernails."

★ Air Anthem:

"Anyway Anyhow Anywhere"

The Who

single, 1965

ANYWAY ANY-OW!

In characteristic style, he promptly went back on his word, with shocking consequences. At the climax of a U.S. show, Townshend windmilled a red Fender Eric Clapton Model Stratocaster with a ferocity sufficient to impale his right hand on the whammy bar. He fainted and was rushed to the hospital. "It was horrendous," observed Roger Daltrey, "We all felt it." Townshend later drolly recalled worrying about all the things he would no longer be able to do with his right hand. Happily, however, the bar missed his nerves or tendons, and the bandaged axeman went straight back to work.

LEVEL:

Amateur Axeman

Townshend's arc de triomphe

Incredibly, he was still at it two decades later. "Townshend has been moaning lately that he's too old to pull off his classic windmill maneuver," wrote Sean Daly of the *St. Petersburg Times* in 2010. "But during his band's 12-minute Super Bowl gig . . . the 64-year-old gunslinger busted out that guitar swipe so many times, I thought his arm would sail into the stands. At the end of 'Who Are You' . . . Townshend was windmilling so hard (and putting some nice raw tone into his licks), he could have powered small nations."

In all, then, a dramatic and easily imitated air guitar move (lean back for maximum dramatic effect). Just watch out for repetitive strain injury.

Ensure feet are planted firmly on terra firma to avoid takeoff

MOUNTING THE MONITOR

Iron Maiden have contributed much to rock iconography, from their ubiquitous logo to the endlessly reincarnated mascot Eddie. Oddly, however, air guitarists can't derive much of use from long-standing string-slingers Dave Murray and Adrian Smith, whose stage moves essentially consist of standing still and playing (albeit playing some of metal's most influential riffs). And imitating "new boy" Janick Gers' tricks—hurling his instrument into the air or spinning it round his neck, and high-kicking round the stage—will look, sans guitar, like interpretive dance. (And Kate Bush you are *not*.)

We must therefore boldly go to singer Bruce Dickinson and founding father and bassist Steve Harris, and their distinctive yet easily imitated use of monitors. It's little wonder that Dickinson and Harris spend so much time on these stage-front units: at five foot six and five foot eight and a half, respectively, they're the shortest in Maiden's six-man line-up. (Perhaps that's why they hide the tallest—six-footer Nicko McBrain—behind rock's most overstuffed drum kit.)

★ Air Anthem:

"The Trooper"

Iron Maiden
Rock in Rio, 2002

LEVEL:
★ ★
Amateur Axeman

MONITOR MADNESS

Dickinson teeters on the monitors, occasionally sits on them to introduce a song, and hurdles them for dramatic effect (not to mention comedic effect, when he lands on his backside). Harris, meanwhile, plants one foot on a monitor, leans forward like a boxer challenging an unfriendly crowd, and snarls along with his own lyrics. Then, if you're lucky, he'll draw his bass to his chest and "machine gun" the audience. None more metal!

All this can be yours with just a sturdy box, a small stool, or a "step" from your mom's aerobics class. For authenticity, remember that Harris delivers his super-speedy bass lines without a plectrum, and that Dickinson—a fencer and a pilot when he's not singing—probably has better coordination than you. The publishers of this book accept no liability for when you fall on your face or smash your coccyx.

35

★THE DUCK WALK★

"Even on a bad night," Angus Young informed *Guitar World,* **"Chuck Berry is a lot better than Clapton will ever be."** Fittingly, the livewire AC/DC figurehead has proved to be the greatest exponent of a move that Berry popularized (rock historians credit T-Bone Walker with its actual invention): moving forward while **"stooping with full-bended knees, but with my back and head vertical."**

Berry—who, with Little Richard, essentially created rock 'n' roll—showcased the move at a show in New York. He and his band members had each brought along just one suit to wear. "We didn't know we were supposed to change," he recalled. "We wanted to do something different, so I actually did that duck walk to hide the wrinkles in the suit—I got an ovation, so I figured I pleased the audience. So I did it again." A reviewer branded the move the duck walk, and the choreography quickly became iconic.

String-slingers from Johnny Thunders to Jimmy Page have imitated it—even Rory Gallagher practiced an athletic variant, with his guitar held at arm's length—though none for so long nor as successfully as Angus Young. (There's even a Facebook page called Angus Young's Duck Walk.)

Chuck Berry: the original duck

LEVEL: ★★★
Master Axeman

QUACK! QUACK!

DOING AN ANGUS

To "do an Angus," first lower your hips as if trying to sit down, then begin moving forward while keeping your weight on your heels. Raise one knee, then bring it down while jumping forward with the other leg. It's harder than it looks!

Once you've mastered that, why not try more of the metal madman's moves? There's the close-kneed shuffle across the stage, imitated by Jack White and Green Day's Billie Joe Armstrong. And there's the "spasm": falling on your back, then kicking and spinning around. We would, however, advise against Angus-style dropping of pants, unless you're sure that you've judged your audience correctly.

★ Air Anthem:

"Riff Raff"
AC/DC
If You Want Blood You've Got It, 1978

37

THE HENDRIX

Hendrix first wowed British audiences—including Jeff Beck and Pete Townshend—in 1966, aged just twenty-three. His stage act was jaw-dropping: The once-shocking long hair of the Rolling Stones was nothing compared to a near-six-foot black man with fancy frills, 'fro, and fretwork. Classic cuts like "Purple Haze" and "Little Wing" set standards for music from psychedelia to twenty-first-century blues; it would take another decade, and the emergence of Eddie Van Halen, to so completely transform the art of guitar. So amateurs need not apply: Hendrix is strictly for air guitarists with plenty of practice under their bullet belts. And take a tip from the great man himself: "In this life, you gotta do what you want. You gotta let your mind and fancy flow, flow, flow free."

Air Anthem:

"The Star-Spangled Banner (live at Woodstock)"

Experience Hendrix:
The Best of Jimi Hendrix, 2010

THE XXX FACTOR

"Most sexual thing I've seen for a long time!" enthused Mick Jagger about Hendrix's stage act in 1967. Let us be blunt: Your guitar is groin-powered and your audience is panting for it. Cultivate that "I could impregnate you with my music alone" aura.

LEVEL:
Master Axeman

LEFt IS RIGHt

Like many a string-driven legend—from Paul McCartney and Tony Iommi to Kurt Cobain and Omar Rodríguez López—Hendrix played left-handed. Make sure you remember that, or you'll be laughed offstage quicker than you can say "Billy Ray Cyrus."

DON't PLAY It StRAIGHt

Hendrix revolutionized rock by ripping up the rule book. He rubbed his thumb along the low E string in a frankly masturbatory fashion, he used the back of his hand as an impromptu slide . . . Go nuts, but go with what feels *oh so right* (see The XXX Factor, left).

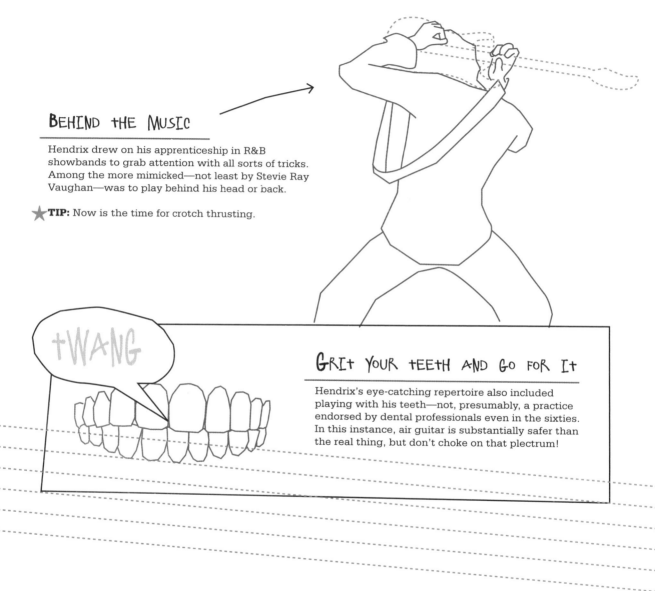

BEHIND THE MUSIC

Hendrix drew on his apprenticeship in R&B showbands to grab attention with all sorts of tricks. Among the more mimicked—not least by Stevie Ray Vaughan—was to play behind his head or back.

★ **TIP:** Now is the time for crotch thrusting.

tWANG

GRIt YOUR tEEtH AND GO FOR It

Hendrix's eye-catching repertoire also included playing with his teeth—not, presumably, a practice endorsed by dental professionals even in the sixties. In this instance, air guitar is substantially safer than the real thing, but don't choke on that plectrum!

DRESS tHE PARt

When working for Little Richard, Hendrix was told, "I am the only one allowed to be pretty. Take off those shirts." But when leading his own band, Hendrix let his wardrobe run as wild as his fretwork. T-shirt and trainers won't cut it: think Sgt. Pepper meets Phil Lynott.

Let me stand next to your . . . oops

IT MAY HAVE BEEN HENDRIX'S MOST SHOWSTOPPING STUNT, BUT UNDER NO CIRCUMSTANCES SHOULD YOU SET FIRE TO YOUR AIR GUITAR.

REMEMBER: YOU ARE PLAYING AN IMAGINARY INSTRUMENT, SO YOU WOULD BE POURING LIGHTER FUEL ON YOUR FLOOR AND IGNITING IT—RARELY A GOOD IDEA.

★JUMP!★

Putting air between your soles and terra firma is an established part of rock 'n' roll, as anyone who's ever pogoed, moshed, or, indeed, listened to House of Pain's "Jump Around" will testify. (Not to mention Kris Kross's "Jump" and the Pointer Sisters' "Jump for My Love." However, as splendid as these undoubtedly are, you'd be hard-pressed to air guitar to either of them.)

READY . . .

Jumping is associated more with audiences than with performers. But it has been dramatically deployed by a variety of axemen, from Billie Joe Armstrong and Mike Dirnt of Green Day to Paul Stanley of Kiss and Pete Townshend—who, as Eddie Vedder noted, could often be seen "leaping into the rafters wielding a seventies Gibson Les Paul, which happens to be a stunningly heavy guitar."

The Townshend move that has become a Green Day trademark is the "tucked knees against stomach" special. Note that your arms need to be outstretched in order to avoid smashing your guitar (whether real or imaginary) against your kneecaps (real, we trust).

LEVEL: ★ ★ ★
Master Axeman

Air Anthem:

"Panama"

Van Halen
1984, 1984

GEt SEt . . .

Paul Stanley's repertoire includes a splayed-leg star jump (easily accomplished with air guitar, although you may look ridiculous) and, more ambitiously, a leap with arched back, knees behind and axe to the fore. The challenge is to overcome the ludicrousness of the maneuver—this is Kiss, after all—and to ensure a graceful, injury-free descent and landing.

JUMP!

The Jedi Knight of jumping is Eddie Van Halen. Not to be outdone by front man David Lee Roth's kung fu high-kicks, EVH developed a quite astonishing "one leg forward, one leg back" leap that barely interrupted his six-string flow. Eddie, we salute you.

However, as poster "Happy Sinner" sagely warned on unsignedbandweb.com: "Check the height of the ceiling over the stage before you do any of this jumping shit in public."

43

CATGUT FEVER

As anyone who has compared the sound of the Foo Fighters to that of Hüsker Dü will testify, there's only so much you can do with a guitar. Some are content to accept these limitations, while others invent a whole new vocabulary. Think of Hendrix, playing as if the guitar were—let's be frank—an intergalactic penis. Think of Dave Gilmour accidentally plugging in his wah-wah backward and creating the distorted seagull cries on Pink Floyd's "Echoes." And then, inevitably, think of Jimmy Page playing his instrument with a violin bow.

★ Air Anthem:

"Vivaldi's 'The Four Seasons' for Violin, Chamber Orchestra & Band"

The Great Kat
Bloody Vivaldi, 1998

LEVEL:

Master Axeman

Let's be honest: It wasn't a brilliant idea musically, as anyone who's sat through a live recording of Zep's "Dazed and Confused" will testify. But as a theatrical device it was a stroke of genius. "The idea was put to me by a classical string player when I was doing studio work," Pagey told *Guitar Player*. "One of us tried to bow the guitar, then we tried it between us, and it worked. At that point I was just bowing it, but other effects I've obviously come up with on my own—using wah-wah and echo. You have to put rosin on the bow, and the rosin sticks to the string and makes it vibrate."

OH, BOW

The idea has been imitated to comic effect—both intentionally and otherwise. In 1984's *This Is Spinal Tap*, Nigel Tufnel plays his guitar not with a bow but with a violin itself. Three years later, Adrian Vandenberg shamelessly mimed with a bow in Whitesnake's "Still of the Night" video—to a part apparently played by Don Airey's keyboards. "I was astonished," Pagey chortled in *Ray Gun*. "I was sitting on the bed watching, and suddenly the guy picks up a bow and I fell off the bed laughing. I just think it's hilarious."

Hilarious or not, the violin bow is easily replicated with a ruler, a novelty fluffy pen or even, well, a violin bow.

SLIIIDE!

When we say "slide," we're not talking about playing slide guitar. You could, if you wished to, imitate Dave Gilmour sitting at a mounted steel guitar, playing as if oblivious to the flashing lights, smoke bombs, and flying pigs around him (see "One of These Days" on the *Pulse* DVD). Or Ronnie Wood, intently studying a metal slide on his fretboard. But shorn of Gilmour's props, you'll look like your grandma, sewing. And minus Woody's slide, it'll look like you're giving the middle finger to your audience—a bad idea, unless you're actually in the Sex Pistols.

FOR THIS SORT OF SLIDE, YOU'LL NEED:

a) space

b) confidence

c) robust knees

It is, as Kyle Gass observes in *Tenacious D and the Pick of Destiny*, "the single most powerful stage move in any rocker's arsenal." Yes, we mean the power slide: hurling yourself across the stage, on your knees.

LEVEL:

Master Axeman

Woo-Who

Matt Bellamy does it, Prince does it (in the *Sign o' the Times* movie, he scoots between dancer Cat's legs and whips her skirt off with his teeth, albeit not with guitar in hand), and even Bruce Springsteen does it. "With surprising acceleration, Bruce sprinted across the stage and went to ground like the Italian National soccer team," marveled sundayhop.com of the E Street Band's 2009 Super Bowl show. "His perfectly oiled pantalons carried him swiftly on his knees towards an unsuspecting cameraman. The producer . . . cut to the camera just in time to see Bruce sling himself crank-first into America's living rooms."

For near Jedi-like athleticism, however, we must turn once more to Pete Townshend. His power slide at around 7:50 minutes into "Won't Get Fooled Again"—the climax to the Who's fantastic 1979 rockumentary *The Kids Are Alright*—is probably the most famous in pop history. (Roger Daltrey's earsplitting scream helps, admittedly.)

★ Air Anthem:

"Won't Get Fooled Again"

The Who
The Kids are Alright, 1979

But beware: If your jeans are artfully torn, you may burn your knees. Or, worse still, snag yourself on a loose board, come to an abrupt halt, and fall flat on your face.

A BRIEF GUIDE to SOME OTHER

AIR-PUNCHING

The old-school alternative to the postmodern devil horns (see also Devil Horns).

LEVEL:
⭐

Learner

⭐ Air anthem:

🎵 "The Fight Song"

Marilyn Manson

Holy Wood (In the Shadow of the Valley of Death), 2000

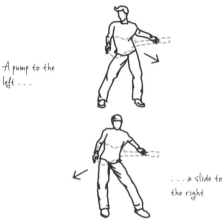

A pump to the left . . .

. . . a slide to the right

THE BOOGIE

Shifting from one hip to another, as if having pleasantly uneventful sexual intercourse (see Legs Akimbo).

🎵 ⭐ Air anthem:

"Bad Boy Boogie"

Mötley Crüe

Girls, Girls, Girls, 1987

LEVEL:
⭐

Learner

MOVES YOU MAY WISH to CONSIDER

THE CROTCH THRUST

Abandon all pretence and simply pretend your guitar is a penis (see Prince), hold your axe away from your crotch and grind lasciviously (see Gene Simmons), or don a loincloth and let the audience's imagination do the rest (see Ted Nugent, but not Manowar—always loud, never sexy).

LEVEL:
Amateur Axeman

Try to avoid throttling yourself

Air anthem:

"Bark at the Moon"

Ozzy Osbourne
Bark at the Moon, 1983

Air anthem:

"Let's Go Crazy"

Prince
Purple Rain, 1984

In . . .

. . . out

HULA HOOP

To add a retro vibe to your display, why not try a maneuver popular in the eighties with the likes of Yngwie, Jake E. Lee, and Steve Vai? To wit: swinging the guitar around your shoulders by the strap. On the plus side, doing this with an air guitar will avoid impaling a bandmate. On the minus, people may think you're being Janick Gers of Iron Maiden.

LEVEL:
Amateur Axeman

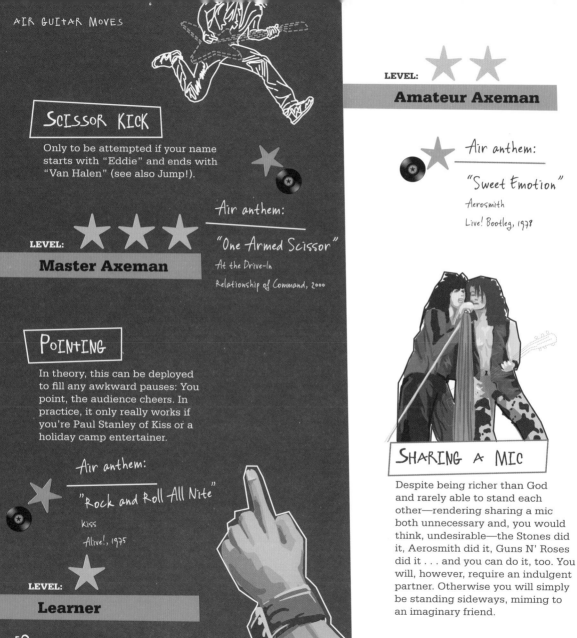

SCISSOR KICK

Only to be attempted if your name starts with "Eddie" and ends with "Van Halen" (see also Jump!).

LEVEL: ★★★
Master Axeman

Air anthem:

"One Armed Scissor"

At the Drive-In

Relationship of Command, 2000

POINTING

In theory, this can be deployed to fill any awkward pauses: You point, the audience cheers. In practice, it only really works if you're Paul Stanley of Kiss or a holiday camp entertainer.

Air anthem:

"Rock and Roll All Nite"

Kiss

Alive!, 1975

LEVEL: ★
Learner

LEVEL: ★★
Amateur Axeman

Air anthem:

"Sweet Emotion"

Aerosmith

Live! Bootleg, 1978

SHARING A MIC

Despite being richer than God and rarely able to stand each other—rendering sharing a mic both unnecessary and, you would think, undesirable—the Stones did it, Aerosmith did it, Guns N' Roses did it . . . and you can do it, too. You will, however, require an indulgent partner. Otherwise you will simply be standing sideways, miming to an imaginary friend.

SHOULDERS

If you're lucky enough to persuade a partner to help you with "sharing a mic" (left), why not ask if they're in the mood for recreating a classic slice of AC/DC stagecraft? Namely: Angus Young being borne through the crowd on the shoulders of Bon Scott, Brian Johnson, or a roadie. Note that gentlemen should probably not request this of wives or girlfriends.

Air anthem:

"Let There Be Rock"
AC/DC
If You Want Blood You've Got It, 1978

LEVEL:
Amateur Axeman

LEVEL:
Amateur Axeman

STRUMMING

It puts the "grrr" in groove. It puts the "mmm" in Molly Hatchet. It's why Guns N' Roses covered "Knockin' on Heaven's Door." It is strumming.

Warning: You will struggle to make this look in any way interesting.

up down
up down –
you get the idea

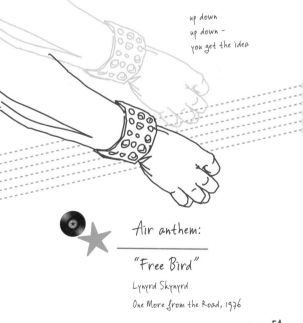

Air anthem:

"Free Bird"
Lynyrd Skynyrd
One More from the Road, 1976

TUNING UP

Only the most anally retentive of air guitarists will feel the need to tune their instrument—which, let us not forget, does not actually exist.

Air anthem:

"Sgt. Pepper's Lonely Hearts Club Band"
The Beatles
Sgt. Pepper's Lonely Hearts Club Band, 1967

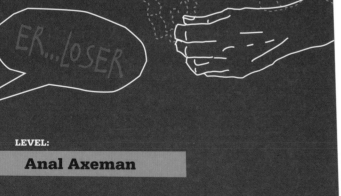

ER...LOSER

LEVEL:

Anal Axeman

LEVEL: ★ ★

Amateur Axman

THE WHIPLASH

Unless you have long hair or a well-secured wig, forget it. But if you do have either of these, tilt your head forward, channel the spirit of Cliff Burton, and windmill your head as if trying to replicate the propeller decapitation scene in *Raiders of the Lost Ark*.

Air anthem:

"Whiplash"
Metallica
Kill 'Em All, 1983

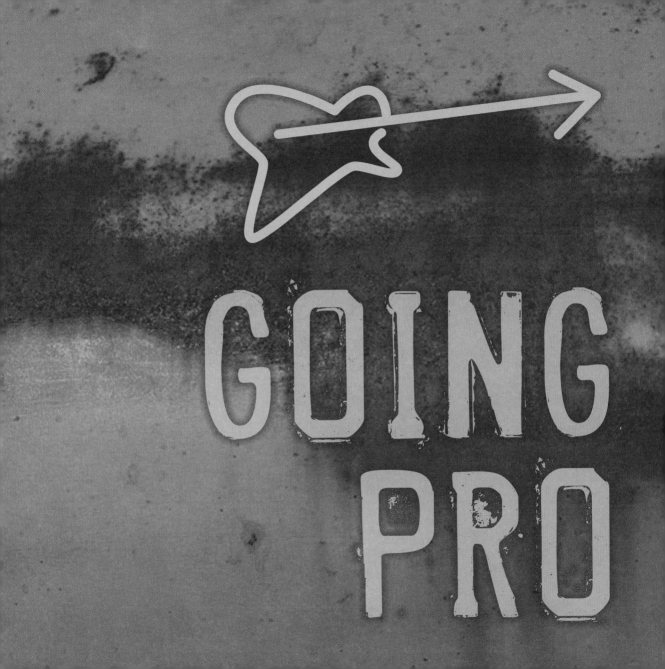

50 FRET-FONDLING FAVORITES

If you're reading this book, no doubt you already have favorite songs that make you dust off that imaginary axe and shake your airy thang. But here are our suggestions, from the obscure to the obvious—although we have observed the *Wayne's World* dictum: "No 'Stairway'!"

1 "Day Tripper"

tHE BEAtLES

(Single, 1965)

"That's mine," bragged John Lennon. "Including the lick, the guitar break, and the whole bit." But whether it's Lennon's lick, or Harrison's short but sweet solo, this gem provides perfect opportunities for air guitar. (Check out Jimi Hendrix's version on the great 1988 collection, *Radio One*.) Other Fab Four fret frazzlers include "I Feel Fine," "A Hard Day's Night," "Helter Skelter," "Revolution," "Sgt. Pepper's Lonely Hearts Club Band (reprise)," "I've Got a Feeling" . . . someone really should write a book about this band.

"HARRISON TAUGHT ME ABOUT SHORT SOLOS AND HOOKS, AND WHAT A HOOK IS. ALL THOSE MID-SIXTIES BEATLES TRACKS—WHETHER IT WAS 'DAY TRIPPER' OR 'TICKET TO RIDE' OR WHATEVER—THEY ALL START WITH A GUITAR LICK THAT YOU WAIT TO COME AROUND AGAIN IN THE CHORUS."
—ELLIOTT EASTON, THE CARS

2 "I Need You"

tHE KINKS

(B-side, 1965)

Back in the days when the Kinks were helping invent heavy metal, and bands chucked great songs away on B-sides of singles (in this instance, "Set Me Free Little Girl"), a soon-to-be guitar hero was just a jobbing session player . . .

"YOU KNOW 'I NEED YOU' BY THE KINKS? I THINK I DID THAT BIT THERE IN THE BEGINNING. I DON'T KNOW WHO REALLY DID FEEDBACK FIRST; IT JUST SORT OF HAPPENED. I DON'T THINK ANYBODY CONSCIOUSLY NICKED IT FROM ANYBODY ELSE; IT WAS JUST GOING ON."—JIMMY PAGE, LED ZEPPELIN

The Quiet One:
Not always quiet

2

Pagey: The gold standard

3

"Stroll On"

tHE YARDBIRDS

Blowup, 1966

The Yardbirds are often all but dismissed as simply the springboard for Clapton, Beck, and Page's careers. But their influence can be heard in bands from Pink Floyd to Aerosmith. This chugging curio is an adaptation of their definitive version of "Train Kept A-Rollin'."

"ONE OF THE FEW PERFORMANCES WITH JEFF BECK AND JIMMY PAGE TOGETHER. IT'S FROM THE SOUNDTRACK TO THE MOVIE *BLOWUP*, IN WHICH THERE'S A CLIP OF THEIR PERFORMANCE—A VERY RARE PIECE."—JOE PERRY, AEROSMITH

4

"Jumpin' Jack Flash"

tHE ROLLING StONES

Single, 1968

Bill Wyman claims that he came up with one of rock's best-known riffs—entirely possible, given the Glimmer Twins' historically ruthless approach to song credits. But it's certainly Keef's show, and one to which air guitarists are drawn like moths to a cigarette lighter waving in the air at a festival.

"TO ME, THAT RIFF IS 'SATISFACTION' BACKWARDS, AND I HEAR IT IN NEARLY EVERY SONG THAT I DO."—KEITH RICHARDS

5

"Heartbreaker"

LED ZEPPELIN

Led Zeppelin II, 1969

"Whole Lotta Love" may be the obvious choice, but "Heartbreaker" is *the* anthem from Zep's first chart-topping album. From the swaggering riff that kicks it off, through the fabulous grinding of gears around 1:22, to the Pagey showcase beginning 2:03 and the climactic jam, it's air guitar nirvana.

"THE SINGER'S A BIT OF A BULLSHIT ARTIST, THERE'S TOO MUCH ECHO AND THE F**KING SOLOS ARE TOO LONG."—MALCOLM YOUNG, AC/DC

Neil: Rules do not apply

7 "21st Century Schizoid Man"

KING CRIMSON

In the Court of the Crimson King, 1969

Metal? Prog? Jazz? King Crimson smashed them all into one seven-minute head-trip. For full authenticity, you'll need to look like guitarist Robert Fripp in his Mad Professor With A Perm incarnation, rather than the well-groomed university lecturer of later years.

"WHEN WE OPENED UP WITH THE CRASH FROM '21ST CENTURY SCHIZOID MAN,' THE IMPRESSION I GOT WAS AS IF A GIANT FOOT HAD STEPPED ON THE AUDIENCE. SCRUNCH! MUCH MORE SCRUNCHY THAN WHEN I FIRST SAW BLACK SABBATH A FEW MONTHS LATER."—ROBERT FRIPP

8 "The Star-Spangled Banner"

JIMI HENDRIX

Live, 1969

Hendrix had etched himself into legend before bringing a dive-bombing take on the USA's national anthem (emulated by Bruce Kulick on Kiss's *Alive III* in 1993) to the Woodstock stage. But this string-bending showcase—fancifully interpreted as a sonic comment on the Vietnam War—was the icing on the guitarist's already astounding cake.

"YOU'RE TALKING ABOUT A GUY WHO PLAYED 'THE STAR-SPANGLED BANNER' BUT IN A WAY THAT SHOWED EXACTLY WHAT IT WAS ABOUT. HE PLAYED IT ON DICK CAVETT'S TV SHOW AND CAVETT SAID IT WAS 'UNORTHODOX.' HENDRIX SAID, 'WELL, IT'S BEAUTIFUL TO ME.'"—PRINCE

6 "Cinnamon Girl"

NEIL YOUNG

Everybody Knows This is Nowhere, 1969

It's tricky to pick just one gem from this maverick axe hero's huge and rewarding back catalogue. But let's go for one with an irresistible riff and a typically idiosyncratic solo—ideal for beginners (hence, presumably, why Courtney Love looted it for "Starbelly" on Hole's debut album *Pretty on the Inside*).

"PROBABLY THE BEST ONE-NOTE GUITAR SOLO EVER . . . NEIL HAS SUCH EXPRESSIVE PLAYING THAT HE CAN PLAY A ONE-NOTE SOLO AND MAKE IT MEMORABLE FOR DECADES, FOR GENERATIONS."—NANCY WILSON, HEART

"Loose"

$\frac{9}{=}$

THE STOOGES

Fun House, 1970

It's possible that Ron Asheton did more than any other guitarist to inspire people who couldn't be bothered to learn how to play like Eric Clapton. And so, just as Stooges frontman Iggy Pop is the Godfather of Punk, Ron is the Archduke of Air Guitar. And note this song's hugely influential E-G-A chord progression, most famously deployed in "Smoke on the Water."

"RON HAS A PARTICULAR GRITTY, SLEAZY SOUND WITH THE GROOVE THAT HE LAYS DOWN . . . THERE IS A LOT OF BLUES IN WHAT RON DID, BUT THERE'S SOMETHING A LOT LOOSER, TOO, AND IT WAS FREER AND IT UTILIZED CHAOS . . . 'I WANNA BE YOUR DOG,' 'TV EYE,' 'LOOSE,' 'DOWN ON THE STREET'. . . THEY'RE ALL AMAZING."—KIM THAYIL, SOUNDGARDEN

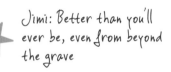

Jimi: Better than you'll ever be, even from beyond the grave

$\frac{10}{=}$

"Highway Star"

DEEP PURPLE

Machine Head, 1972

"Smoke on the Water" will get you laughed offstage, so opt for another one of *Machine Head*'s airworthy anthems. "Highway Star" was conjured after a journalist asked how Purple wrote songs. Ritchie Blackmore duly improvised a riff based on a repeated G on an acoustic guitar—an incongruously low-key birth for this pummeling classic.

"THE FIRST GIG I EVER WENT TO WAS DEEP PURPLE, DURING THEIR *MACHINE HEAD* PERIOD. THEY PLAYED 'HIGHWAY STAR' AND IT BLEW ME AWAY . . . BLACK-MORE'S TECHNIQUE IS GREAT. IT'S AGGRESSIVE. WHEN HE HIT A CHORD, IT WAS LIKE BEING PUNCHED IN THE FACE." —PHIL COLLEN, DEF LEPPARD

11 "Quadrant 4"

BILLY COBHAM

Spectrum, 1973

You may have mastered Eddie Van Halen's "Eruption," but can you twiddle those digits fast enough to be Tommy Bolin on this jazz-rock fusion classic? Although it appears on an album bearing the name of Mahavishnu Orchestra graduate Billy Cobham, this was the track that secured Bolin's place in Deep Purple, and it will make you the world's most nimble-fingered mimic. Or give you arthritis.

"DAVID [COVERDALE] TOLD ME, 'LOOK, YOU'VE GOT TO LISTEN TO THIS' . . . I PUT IT ON AND MY MOUTH DROPPED OPEN."—JON LORD, DEEP PURPLE

Bowie: Not really a pirate

12 "Rebel Rebel"

DAVID BOWIE

Diamond Dogs, 1974

"The ultimate identikit diluted series of computerized rock gestures," sneered writer Nick Kent in the year of its release. "The mechanical Stones riff, the brainless lyrics—real *Nineteen Eighty-Four* rock." It's certainly the most air-tastic item in the Bowie back catalogue.

"IT'S A REAL AIR GUITAR THING, ISN'T IT? I CAN TELL YOU A VERY FUNNY STORY ABOUT THAT. ONE NIGHT, I WAS IN LONDON IN A HOTEL TRYING TO GET SOME SLEEP . . . AND I HEARD THIS RIFF BEING PLAYED REALLY BADLY FROM UPSTAIRS. I THOUGHT, 'WHO THE HELL IS DOING THIS AT THIS TIME OF NIGHT?'—ON AN ELECTRIC GUITAR, OVER AND OVER. SO I WENT UPSTAIRS TO SHOW THE PERSON HOW TO PLAY THE THING [LAUGHS]. I BANG ON THE DOOR. THE DOOR OPENS, AND I SAY, 'LISTEN, IF YOU'RE GOING TO PLAY. . .' AND IT WAS JOHN MCENROE! I KID YOU NOT. IT WAS MCENROE, WHO SAW HIMSELF AS SOME SORT OF ROCK GUITAR PLAYER AT THE TIME. THAT COULD ONLY HAPPEN IN A MOVIE, COULDN'T IT? MCENROE TRYING TO STRUGGLE HIS WAY THROUGH THE 'REBEL REBEL' RIFF."—DAVID BOWIE

"Ogre Battle"

13

QUEEN

Queen II, 1974

When Queen weren't poncing around with opera, music hall, disco, or rockabilly, they were a fantastic hard rock band. Many of these monster moments sprang from Brian May's curly head, such as "We Will Rock You," "Tie Your Mother Down," and "Gimme the Prize." Even Frank Zappa hailed May as "really excellent." This bonkers cut pointed the way forward.

"I DON'T THINK ENOUGH IS REALLY SAID ABOUT THE BRILLIANCE OF BRIAN MAY'S GUITAR PLAYING, IN THE SENSE THAT IT'S OVERSHADOWED BY THE GREATNESS OF THE MUSIC ITSELF. *QUEEN II* . . . JUST NAILED ME TO THE WALL."—STEVE VAI

"Life in the Fast Lane"

14

THE EAGLES

Hotel California, 1976

Hotel California may have done more than any other album to make people welcome punk with open arms. But it did bequeath one of rock's most addictive riffs, with tasty soloing too. Dammit.

"JOE WALSH WAS TUNING HIS GUITAR, AND HE GOES DOODLE-DUDDLE-DUH-DUDDLE-DUH-DUH-DUH. AND I SAID, 'DON [HENLEY, DRUMMER/CO-WRITER], THAT'S "LIFE IN THE FAST LANE." JOE, PLAY THAT LICK AGAIN . . . WE GOTTA USE IT.' SO THAT BECAME THE INTRO, AND THEN I JUST LAID DOWN WHAT WOULD BE CONSIDERED LIKE THE VAMP PROGRESSION FOR THE VERSE, AND WE WERE OFF TO THE RACES."
—GLENN FREY

"American Girl"

15

TOM PETTY AND THE HEARTBREAKERS

Tom Petty and the Heartbreakers, 1976

This jingle-jangle gem was so Byrdsy that Roger McGuinn asked his manager, "When did I write that?" But "American Girl" has become iconic: it popped up in *The Silence of the Lambs* and was ripped off by the Strokes for their "Last Nite."

"A LOT OF ROCK 'N' ROLL SONGS SOUND ALIKE. ASK CHUCK BERRY. THE STROKES TOOK 'AMERICAN GIRL' AND I SAW AN INTERVIEW WITH THEM WHERE THEY ACTUALLY ADMITTED IT. THAT MADE ME LAUGH OUT LOUD. I WAS LIKE, 'OKAY, GOOD FOR YOU.' IT DOESN'T BOTHER ME . . . THERE ARE ENOUGH FRIVOLOUS LAWSUITS IN THIS COUNTRY WITHOUT PEOPLE FIGHTING OVER POP SONGS."
—TOM PETTY

Petty: Not really a girl

16
"Pretty Vacant"

SEX PISTOLS

Never Mind the Bollocks Here's the Sex Pistols, 1977

From Steve Jones' staccato intro to the monstrous riff, "Pretty Vacant" (by bassist Glen Matlock) bolsters Def Leppard singer Joe Elliott's contention that *Never Mind the Bollocks, Here's the Sex Pistols* was a hard rock album with a punk singer.

"TO CUT A LONG STORY SHORT, I WAS SHORT OF A RIFF. ABBA'S 'SOS' CAME ON THE JUKEBOX AND, HEY PRESTO, I HAD IT. BUT YOU'VE GOT TO KNOW WHERE TO LOOK."—GLEN MATLOCK

17
"The Sails of Charon"

THE SCORPIONS

Taken by Force, 1978

Michael "Mad Mickey" Schenker and the long-serving Matthias Jabs may have stolen the limelight, but Uli Jon Roth was the guitarist who really made his mark on the Scorps. Here's one of the reasons why, on his last album with the band.

"AFTER HIS SOLOS, YOU'RE LEFT THERE SHAKING YOUR HEAD. IT'S LIKE BEING SIDESWIPED BY A TRUCK. THE TRACK I LOVE THE MOST IS THE ONE I PLAY EVERY NIGHT, 'THE SAILS OF CHARON' . . . PEOPLE IN THE AUDIENCE WHO KNOW THE SONG RECOGNIZE THAT I'M FLYING THE FLAG FOR THAT OLD SCHOOL METAL, AND THEY COME TO ME AND SAY, BRO, 'SAILS OF CHARON' RULES!"—KIRK HAMMETT, METALLICA

18
"Steal Away the Night"

OZZY OSBOURNE

Blizzard of Ozz, 1980

Air guitarists got down on their knees and thanked the metal gods when the eighties dawned with Randy Rhoads' introduction. "Crazy Train" is the one you see in every poll, but it's "Steal Away (the Night)" that truly captures the joy of his pyrotechnical playing. As with Dimebag Darrell and other greats gone too soon, what greater tribute could there be than putting on Randy's music and bringing him back to life through the medium of mime?

"WHEN OZZY'S *BLIZZARD OF OZZ* CAME OUT, SOME FRIENDS OF MINE WENT TO SEE HIM PERFORM IN OAKLAND AND CAME BACK RAVING, SAYING, 'MAN, WE SAW THIS GUITARIST TODAY, AND HE WAS BETTER THAN EDDIE VAN HALEN!' . . . RANDY WAS DOING EVERYTHING THAT VAN HALEN DID, AND MORE." —FRANK HANNON, TESLA

Randy: Still rockin' in heaven

Malcolm: Mighty midget

20 "Start Me Up"

THE ROLLING STONES

Tattoo You, 1981

The Stones were already elder statesmen three decades ago, yet they blasted into the eighties with this international smash. Originally cut as a reggae number in the late seventies, it was reworked in 1981. The Cult's "Love Removal Machine" is the most blatant of the songs that have ripped it off.

"IT WAS A RIFF THAT MICK BROUGHT ALONG [BUT] IN THE END 'START ME UP' BECAME A MICK AND KEITH-WELDED SONG . . . IT WAS ONE OF THOSE GENUINE COLLABORATIONS BETWEEN THE TWO OF THEM, WITH A LITTLE MAGIC FROM BOTH SIDES."—RONNIE WOOD

19 "Back in Black"

AC/DC

Back in Black, 1980

"Go and listen to the opening chords of 'Back in Black,'" Scott Ian of Anthrax once urged. "If that doesn't move you, then you have no soul." Indeed, this mighty metal motherf**ker—conceived by rhythm guitarist Malcolm Young on the *Highway to Hell* tour—is impossible to sit still to.

"THE RIFF IS SO COOL AND SIMPLE. WHENEVER I HEARD THAT ONE, IT ALWAYS STOPPED ME. IT WAS LIKE A COOL KEITH RICHARDS LICK."—GARY ROSSINGTON, LYNYRD SKYNYRD

21 "Limelight"

RUSH

Moving Pictures, 1981

The Rush catalogue is littered with airworthy moments, from bits of *2112* to virtually all of 1993's *Counterparts*. But "Limelight" is where Alex Lifeson proves once and for all that he can stand tall beside Geddy Lee and Neil Peart, two of rock's finest musicians.

"I LOVE THE ELASTICITY OF THE SOLO. IT'S A VERY EMOTIONAL PIECE OF MUSIC FOR ME TO PLAY. THE SONG IS ABOUT LONELINESS AND ISOLATION, AND I THINK THE SOLO REFLECTS THAT. THERE'S A LOT OF HEART IN IT. EVEN NOW IT'S MY FAVORITE SOLO TO PERFORM LIVE. I NEVER GET TIRED OF IT." —ALEX LIFESON

"Photograph"

23

DEF LEPPARD

Pyromania, 1983

One of Steve "Steamin'" Clark's more Stonesy riffs (see also "Armageddon It" on 1986's *Hysteria*) powers this immortal ode to a picture of Marilyn Monroe that once hung on the inside of singer Joe Elliott's bathroom door. Carlos Santana has covered the song.

"I NEEDED TO MAKE 'PHOTOGRAPH' DANCE LIKE PUERTO RICAN WOMEN. IT WASN'T JUST A NORMAL DANCE. SO I HAD TO MESS WITH IT A LOT MORE, WHILE ALSO RESPECTING WHERE IT CAME FROM . . . I LIKE TO PLEASE THE WOMEN, SO WE HAD TO CHANGE THE BED."—CARLOS SANTANA

"Beat It"

22

MICHAEL JACKSON

Thriller, 1982

The gem that made eighties pop kids take up air guitar, thanks to an addictive riff by Toto's Steve Lukather. And as if that wasn't good enough, it had a searing solo by Eddie Van Halen. Bonus fact #1: Eddie joined the Jacksons onstage at the Texas Stadium on July 14, 1984, to play the song. Bonus fact #2: an Ernie Ball Music Man EVH guitar is played by Macaulay Culkin in Jackson's "Black or White" video.

"THE FIRST TIME I HEARD EDDIE VAN HALEN WAS ON THE SOLO FOR MICHAEL JACKSON'S 'BEAT IT.' I WAS LIKE, 'MAN, THAT'S UNBELIEVABLE. WHO IS THIS GUITAR PLAYER?' . . . AFTER THAT I JUST REALLY WANTED TO PLAY LIKE HIM."—RICHIE KOTZEN, POISON/MR. BIG

Eddie and Michael:
Beat that, suckers

24

"Rock You Like a Hurricane"

THE SCORPIONS

Love at First Sting, 1984

"There's too many heavy metal bands," complained Scorpions singer Klaus Meine in 1984, "that are just boring with all their monsters and all this shit." With the assistance of drummer Herman "Ze German" Rarebell and guitarist Rudy Schenker, Meine duly conjured this *Dungeons and Dragons*–free blend of simple but timeless power chords that, over a quarter of a century later, can be heard everywhere from sports stadiums to *The Simpsons*.

"WE ARE STILL READY TO MAKE GOOD MUSIC, KICK ASSES AND ROCK YOU LIKE A HURRICANE!"—RUDY SCHENKER

Mark: None more metal

25

"Partytime (Zombie Version)"

45 GRAVE

The Return of the Living Dead soundtrack, 1985

Proto-goths from the City of Angels, 45 Grave—led by the brilliantly stage-named Dinah Cancer—were naturals for the soundtrack of Dan O'Bannon's horror classic. They duly exhumed a gem from their debut album and gave it a blockbusting makeover. If zombies could play air guitar, this is what they'd play.

"45 GRAVE ARE MY ALL-TIME FAVORITE ROCK BAND. THEY INCLUDED MEMBERS OF THE GERMS AND THE GUN CLUB. THIS SONG SOUNDS LIKE ALICE COOPER—ONLY *GOOD*."
—RYAN ADAMS

26

"Money for Nothing"

DIRE STRAITS

Brothers in Arms, 1985

The riff that, over a quarter of a century ago, turned the entire population of the world into air guitarists.

"MOST PEOPLE GOT THE JOKE, BUT I THINK THERE'S CERTAINLY SOME WHO JUST LIKED THE GUITAR RIFF AND DIDN'T NECESSARILY LISTEN TO THE WORDS."
—MARK KNOPFLER

Jeff: Easier to spell than Yngwie

"I'll See the Light, Tonight"

27

YNGWIE MALMSTEEN'S RISING FORCE

Marching Out, 1985

Rick Nielsen playing a five-necked guitar? Justin Hawkins soloing on the back of a flying stuffed tiger? Steve Vai joining Whitesnake? Pah, amateurs! We all know that, in the guitar lexicon, "bonkers" is spelled Y-N-G-W-I-E.

"YNGWIE IS ONE OF THOSE PLAYERS THAT HAD A HUGE IMPACT ON ME. HIS NEOCLASSICAL STYLE WAS JUST MIND-BLOWING TO ME . . . JUST THE FEROCITY OF IT WAS MESMERIZING. THE EASE WITH WHICH HE DOES IT WAS FASCINATING, TOO."— GEORGE LYNCH, DOKKEN/LYNCH MOB

"Wild Thing"

28

JEFF BECK

Single, 1986

The Troggs' U.S. chart-topping 1966 gem had been endlessly covered—not least by Jimi Hendrix—in the two decades before Jeff Beck got his hands on it. He, however, subjected the song to a proto-industrial makeover that amped up its menace but sacrificed none of its swagger. Winningly, this version—available on 1991's indispensable *Beckology*—ends with a snippet of *The Troggs Tapes*.

"SINCE HE CAME TO PROMINENCE IN THE YARDBIRDS, HE IS STILL THE ONLY PERSON PUSHING FORWARD IN THAT WAY. HE'S NEVER RETREADING OLD GROUND; HE'S ALWAYS LOOKING FOR A NEW CHALLENGE. JEFF'S SCARILY BRILLIANT." —DAVID GILMOUR, PINK FLOYD

29

"No Sleep Till Brooklyn"

BEASTIE BOYS

Licensed to Ill, 1986

Title adapted from Motörhead? Check. Riff looted from AC/DC's "TNT"? Check. Pastiche solo from Slayer's Kerry King? Check. Air guitar anthem? Affirmative.

"I JUST WENT IN AND DID SOMETHING, OUT OF TUNE."
—KERRY KING, SLAYER

30

"Master of Puppets"

METALLICA

Master of Puppets, 1986

The connoisseur's choice from the 'tallica album catalogue is jam-packed with air-worthy anthems, from the acoustic opening of "Battery" to the brutal "Damage, Inc." But its highlight is the title track, complete with sky-crashing-down intro riffs, a soaring twin-guitar breakdown, and a widdly solo.

"SOMETIMES WE LOOK BACK AT A LOT OF OUR MATERIAL AND WONDER HOW—OR WHY—WE EVER CAME UP WITH CERTAIN PARTS. OR WONDER WHY WE JUST DIDN'T TURN CERTAIN RIFFS INTO THEIR OWN SONGS, BECAUSE THEY WERE SO GOOD."—JAMES HETFIELD

"Angel of Death"

31

SLAYER

Reign in Blood, 1986

"SLAYER! SLAYER! SLAYER!" If this invocation has never left your lips, what are you even doing reading this book?

"I [ONLY] JUST STARTED GETTING INTO THEM BECAUSE I WAS PRETTY MUCH AT ODDS WITH THOSE GUYS FOR SO LONG. I'D HAVE TO SAY MY FAVORITE SONG IS 'ANGEL OF DEATH'."—DAVE MUSTAINE, MEGADETH

Hetfield and Hammett: Titans of 'tallica

32
"Dr. Feelgood"
MÖTLEY CRÜE

Dr. Feelgood, 1989

There was much to admire about the Crüe's greatest album, not least a power-house sound that led Metallica to recruit *Dr. Feelgood* producer Bob Rock for their "Black Album." But most notable was the title track, cowritten by guitarist Mick Mars. He left a Zeppelin-sized stamp, from the opening squalls to the closing riffing, and the result was Mötley's biggest hit. For an authentic performance, you'll need to air guitar in a tent in a desert, surrounded by flames. And don't spare the hairspray.

"MICK IS ABSOLUTELY THE GROUP'S MUSICAL HEARTBEAT."
—VINCE NEIL

33
"Always on the Run"
LENNY KRAVITZ

Mama Said, 1991

Fooling around with a riff that he hadn't been able to use in Guns N' Roses, Slash conjured this badass groove. Air guitar judges should, we say, award you credit for not choosing the yawningly obvious "Are You Gonna Go My Way."

"IT WAS A LOT OF FUN—VERY RAW AND STRIPPED DOWN, THE WAY IT SHOULD BE DONE."—SLASH

34
"Enter Sandman"
METALLICA

Metallica, 1991

Bamboozled by having to recreate 1988's ambitious . . . *And Justice for All* onstage, Metallica shed their prog trappings for the new decade. Leading the charge was what drummer Lars Ulrich hailed as "the most straightforward, simplest song we had ever written." Now as much a part of metal DNA as "Whole Lotta Rosie," "Whole Lotta Love," and "Crazy Horses," "Enter Sandman" practically demands that you air guitar along, rocking back and forth Status Quo-style.

"SOUNDGARDEN HAD JUST PUT OUT *LOUDER THAN LOVE*. I WAS TRYING TO CAPTURE THEIR ATTITUDE TOWARD BIG, HEAVY RIFFS."—KIRK HAMMETT

Mick: Could probably use a doctor

McCready: Hats sure are handy in Seattle

36 "Cannonball"

THE BREEDERS

Last Splash, 1993

Her Pixies back catalogue is littered with songs that made the meekest of men air guitar themselves into a frenzy, but Kim Deal really hit the bull's-eye with this indie perennial. The bass provides the lolloping groove, but the grinding guitar makes it explode—a trick to which Jonny Greenwood must have paid attention when Radiohead were assembling "Paranoid Android."

"I WAS BORROWING MY BROTHER'S HARMONICA MICROPHONE AND SCREAMING AT A MARSHALL AMPLIFIER. PEOPLE ENJOYED IT AND SO THAT'S GREAT."—KIM DEAL

"Alive"

35 PEARL JAM

Ten, 1991

"Even Flow," "Jeremy," and "Black" were three of the classics that helped propel Pearl Jam's debut album to greater sales than archrivals Nirvana's *Nevermind*. But most irresistible to fret-fondlers is "Alive." Mike McCready's epic guitar solo kicks in at about the 3:39 mark and continues for two thrilling minutes. Proof that his formative years of "leaping around the couch with brooms and in front of the mirror" had really paid off.

"I COPIED ACE FREHLEY'S SOLO FROM [KISS'] 'SHE,' WHICH WAS COPIED FROM ROBBY KRIEGER'S SOLO IN THE DOORS' 'FIVE TO ONE'."—MIKE MCCREADY

Zakk: Wylde by name . . .

37 "Big Love"

FLEETWOOD MAC

The Dance, 1997

If you want to display your dexterity, you can tackle "Eruption" by Van Halen or "White Knuckles" by Gary Moore (or, if you're completely insane, ex-Kiss man Vinnie Vincent's 71-minute "Speedball Jamm"). However, if you really want to show off, try replicating Lindsey Buckingham's super-speedy Spanish guitar-esque version of this *Tango in the Night* hit. Warning: you may need twice as many fingers as you actually have.

"'BIG LOVE' [GETS] CLOSE TO THE APPROACH THAT I'M INTERESTED IN DOING NOW, WHICH IS TO GET MAYBE ONE OR TWO GUITARS TO DO THE WORK OF A WHOLE TRACK—OR TO DO MORE EXPERIMENTAL FINGER-PICKING THINGS."
—LINDSEY BUCKINGHAM

38 "DNR (Do Not Resuscitate)"

TESTAMENT

The Gathering, 1999

While Metallica were recruiting the San Francisco Symphony orchestra and going all Pink Floyd, another group of West Coast brain-bashers were proving that thrash metal was not, in fact, moribund. For this one, your hands will need to blur to keep up with Dave Lombardo's Energizer Bunny drumming—but your audience might not notice, as this song will blow their heads off.

"'DNR' JUST ROCKS ON. WHERE WOULD YOU PUT A SOLO? THE RHYTHMS *ARE* PRETTY MUCH A SOLO."—ERIC PETERSON

39 "All for You"

BLACK LABEL SOCIETY

Stronger than Death, 2000

If you didn't already know Zakk Wylde had made a name for himself playing Black Sabbath and Randy Rhoads riffs with Ozzy Osbourne, this very metal monster should tip you off.

"YOU KNOW RIGHT AWAY THAT IT'S HIM, WITH THAT DISTINCTIVE USE OF HARMONIC VIBRATO ON THE LOWER STRING. BEFORE HE CAME ALONG, EVERY TIME YOU SAW A BLOND-HAIRED GUITARIST KICKING A LES PAUL'S ASS, YOU THOUGHT OF JOHN SYKES. NOW YOU ALSO THINK OF ZAKK."
—RON 'BUMBLEFOOT' THAL, GUNS N' ROSES

Bellamy: Shy and retiring

40

"Plug In Baby"

MUSE

Origin of Symmetry, 2001

"Almost instantly recognizable for its use of a rising triad motif to move through a distinctively classical minor scale," said *Total Guitar*. No, we don't know what that means, either—but *TG* readers voted this the best riff of the twenty-first century, and presumably they know what they're talking about.

"I THINK THE CHORUS IS PROBABLY REFERRING TO SOME KIND OF ANALOGY OF THE TOURING LIFESTYLE, OF WHAT IT FEELS LIKE BEING ON STAGE . . . BUT KIND OF SAYING THAT, REALLY, I'M PREPARED TO PRETTY MUCH SACRIFICE EVERYTHING IN MY PERSONAL LIFE FOR THE SAKE OF PLAYING MUSIC."—MATT BELLAMY

41

"Just a Day"

FEEDER

Single, 2001

Brit trio Feeder have amassed an array of anthems—see the 2006 hits set *The Singles* for proof. But "Just a Day" deserves special mention for its heartwarming video, featuring young fans miming, dancing, drinking tea, and, yes, air guitaring to the song.

"IT'S THE SIMPLE SONGS THAT CONNECT WITH PEOPLE . . . YOU END UP THINKING, 'WELL, I'VE WRITTEN MUCH BETTER SONGS, BUT NOBODY GIVES A SHIT ABOUT THOSE.'"
—GRANT NICHOLAS

43

"I Believe in a Thing Called Love"

THE DARKNESS

Single, 2002

Let's face it: if you're playing air guitar, you've embraced the notion of inherent ludicrousness. And there's no better soundtrack to shameless stupidity than The Darkness.

"IT'S JUST SPINAL TAP, ISN'T IT? . . . I DON'T GET IT AT ALL."
—JON BON JOVI

"Fell in Love with a Girl"

42 THE WHITE STRIPES

White Blood Cells, 2001

"Let's break this down as much as possible," Jack White said of the White Stripes' *modus operandi,* "and have it still be rock 'n' roll and show what two people can do." Rarely was that better realized than on this frenzied hit—and, as it took only two people, one air guitarist shouldn't have too much of a struggle.

"THERE'S A MALE AND A FEMALE, AND THERE'S THREE COMPONENTS OF THE MUSIC, OVER AND OVER AGAIN."
—JACK WHITE

Jack: White, but not stripey

Justin: Jon Bon Jovi doesn't get him

No 44 "Beast and the Harlot"

AVENGED SEVENFOLD

City of Evil, 2005

While "Bat Country" was *City of Evil*'s biggest hit, air guitarists couldn't stop hitting Repeat on its opening song. (Note that, like Marilyn Manson, Synyster Gates is not his real name—he began life as Brian Haner. You just *know* that both of them played air guitar before they got famous.)

"I BOUGHT EVERY SINGLE LED ZEPPELIN ALBUM, TRIED TO TRANSCRIBE THEM AND LEARN JIMMY PAGE'S SOLOS. I WAS BLOWN AWAY AT THE TIME BY HOW HE WROTE, PLAYED AND PRODUCED ALL THAT SHIT."—SYNYSTER GATES

No 45 "B.Y.O.B."

SYSTEM OF A DOWN

Mezmerize, 2005

System of a Down set a new benchmark for air guitar with 2001's *Toxicity*. Then they topped even that album's Molotov cocktail of infectious riffs and weird time signatures with this explosive smash. Its near-perfect blend of strumming and solos will defy your audience to stay still.

"I MIGHT BE THE MAIN SONGWRITER IN THIS BAND BUT EVERYBODY HAS A SAY . . . I DON'T GIVE A DAMN WHO THOUGHT OF IT, AS LONG AS THE SONG COMES OUT—AS LONG AS IT'S A SONG THAT'S GONNA HAVE CHARACTER, STAND UP ON ITS OWN TWO FEET."—DARON MALAKIAN

"The Dark Eternal Night"

DREAM THEATER

Systematic Chaos, 2007

This teeters on the brink of prog, threatening to topple over entirely when Jordan Rudess's horrible keyboard solo kicks in. Otherwise, it's a showcase for John Petrucci's Mudvayne-inspired riffing and shredding. Only after mastering this should you attempt anything by The Mars Volta.

"WHAT I WANTED TO DO . . . WAS JUST HAVE A CLASSIC HEAVY RIFF. THERE ARE CERTAIN IDENTIFIABLE RIFFS, WHEN YOU'RE PLAYING IN CONCERT, WHERE YOU START THE RIFF AND PEOPLE JUST KINDA GO NUTS. SO THAT SONG IS PROBABLY JUST ABOUT AS HEAVY AS ANY SONG WE'VE DONE." —JOHN PETRUCCI

"Through the Fire and Flames"

DRAGONFORCE

Inhuman Rampage, 2006

If a sonic smoothie of Bon Jovi and Pantera doesn't make you run for the hills—or double over laughing—this is a full-blast weedly-wee workout. And if you've ascended through all the levels of *Rock Band* or *Guitar Hero*, "Through the Fire and Flames" is your final challenge.

"WHAT'S COOLER THAN HAVING THE HARDEST SONG EVER ON *GUITAR HERO*?"—HERMAN LI

Li and Petrucci: Guitar heroes

48

"Halo"

MACHINE HEAD

The Blackening, 2007

With four of its cuts—including this—weighing in at over nine minutes, Machine F**king Head's fantastic, career-reviving *The Blackening* has plenty for Long-Distance Air Guitarists to get their fingers into.

"IT'S NOT TOOL HIPPIE SPACE JAM FOR TEN MINUTES AND IT'S NOT 30 RIFFS THAT ARE GOING NOWHERE, JUST RIFF SOUP. IT'S STILL A SONG IN THE CLASSIC POP SENSE OF WHAT A SONG IS: IT'S GOT A BRIDGE AND A CHORUS AND A VERSE. IT'S GOT THESE THREADS OF CONSISTENCY THAT WEAVE THROUGHOUT THE SONG . . . LIKE, 'OH YEAH, THAT PART.' AND, IN BETWEEN THOSE PARTS, WE'VE TAKEN YOU ON A ROLLERCOASTER RIDE, BUT WE'LL BRING YOU BACK AND THAT'S WHAT COOL."—ROBB FLYNN

49

"Waking the Demon"

BULLET FOR MY VALENTINE

Scream Air Fire, 2008

If you've ever been mocked for playing air guitar, check out the video to this song. Michael Paget's solo will make you turn into a werewolf (apparently) *and then you'll really show 'em!*

"IT'S ABOUT GETTING REVENGE ON A BULLY AT SCHOOL BY SLICING PIECES OFF. THERE'S SOME REALLY SICK SHIT IN THERE, SO I'M HAPPY."—MATT TUCK

"When You Were Young"

50 THE KILLERS

Live from the Royal Albert Hall, 2009

"Mr. Brightside" is the best known of Dave Keuning's riffs, but the ones that betrayed an adolescence spent air guitaring were the expansive "When You Were Young" and the grinding "All the Pretty Faces," the A and B sides of the first *Sam's Town* hit. The over-the-top onstage incarnation of the former is captured on the band's 2009 live album.

"WHEN YOU'RE IN EIGHTH GRADE, YOU'RE INTO AC/DC AND METALLICA. AND ANY GUITARIST WHO SAYS THEY WEREN'T IS F**KING LYING."—DAVE KEUNING

Paget: Not really a werewolf

DON'T TRY THESE AT HOME!

10 ROCK CLASSICS THAT NO AIR GUITARIST SHOULD ATTEMPT

"Sweet Child O' Mine"

GUNS N' ROSES

Appetite for Destruction, 1987

As *Esquire* sagely noted when it named Slash "Best Guitarist" in 2005, "He's who we see ourselves as every time we strap on an air guitar. The top hat. The hair. The dangling cigarette. The near-death experiences." It is certainly true that the one-time GNR axeman has been responsible for many a six-string gem, such as the Grammy-winning Velvet Revolver hit "Slither." However, the riff that put him—and Guns N' Roses—on the map is so extraordinarily fiddly that, were you to attempt it, your fingers would fall off by the end of the opening bars.

"I HAVE A WAY OF SITTING DOWN WITH THE GUITAR AND COMING UP WITH THESE HARD-TO-PLAY RIFFS; THEY'RE UNORTHODOX FINGERINGS OF SIMPLE MELODIES."
—SLASH

Try this instead: "New Rose" (*The Spaghetti Incident?*, 1993)

"Shine On You Crazy Diamond"

PINK FLOYD

Wish You Were Here, 1975

This stone-cold classic has some of Dave Gilmour's most breathtakingly beautiful guitar: a true tour de force of Peter Green–esque melancholy. However, it goes on for ages and is glacially slow, so you won't be air guitaring so much as standing around and occasionally wiggling your fingers, like a bewildered mountaineer rescued from an icy peak.

"PSYCHEDELIA AND BLUES COMING TOGETHER IS OBVIOUSLY A LARGE PART OF WHAT I DO."—DAVE GILMOUR

Try this instead: "Young Lust" (*The Wall*, 1979)

Slash: Fiddly

"Tubular Bells"

MIKE OLDFIELD

Tubular Bells, 1973

The clue is in the title. Yes, it's dead sinister and, yes, it was the theme for *The Exorcist*. But can you wait nearly seven minutes for a really cool guitar bit to show up?

"MOST OF IT IS PRETTY ATROCIOUS. THE TEXTURES ARE SHARP AND EDGY. THE PLAYING IS FUMBLED EVERYWHERE, BITS ARE PLAYED WITHOUT EMOTION AND, WELL, IT'S JUST A FIRST ATTEMPT."—MIKE OLDFIELD

Try this instead: "Hergest Ridge, part 2" (*Hergest Ridge*, 1974)

"Livin' on a Prayer"

BON JOVI

Slippery When Wet, 1987

Signature song for JBJ & Co. it may be (although Jon initially feared it wasn't good enough to go on his band's breakthrough album)—and "Livin' on a Prayer" can, admittedly, be found on games in both the *Guitar Hero* and *Rock Band* franchises. But the Richie Sambora contribution that everyone remembers isn't his guitar playing, it's his talkbox. And if you try to replicate that, you won't look like you're air guitaring. You'll look like you're having a stroke.

"THAT THING IS NOT VERY EASY TO PLAY. BASICALLY, EVERYTHING GETS FED THROUGH A ONE-INCH TUBE THAT GOES IN YOUR MOUTH. THEN YOU TRY TO SING THROUGH IT . . . I TRIED IT ONCE. IT WILL DAMN NEAR TAKE YOUR FACE OFF. YOUR EYEBALLS ARE BEING DISLODGED FROM THEIR SOCKETS."—JON BON JOVI

Try this instead: "Raise Your Hands" (*Slippery When Wet*, 1986)

"Fool to Cry"

THE ROLLING STONES

Black and Blue, 1976

A possibly apocryphal tale has Keith Richards falling asleep while playing this mournful beauty onstage in Frankfurt in 1976. (A review of the show in the British music paper *Sounds*, however, noted: "Keith is exemplary, building on a very precise wah-wah.") Reader: you are not the invincible Keith Richards. You are an air guitarist. Take this as a warning.

"IT IS A VERY BORING SONG AND I WAS PRETTY OUT OF IT. I WAS ON ONE OF THOSE VOLUME PEDALS AND I JUST STAYED ON IT—BUT IT GOT SO LOUD THAT I HAD TO WAKE UP."—KEITH RICHARDS

Try this instead: "Brown Sugar" (*Sticky Fingers*, 1971)

"Heaven and Hell"

BLACK SABBATH

Heaven and Hell, 1980

Despite the unmistakable stamp of the quintessential heavy metal guitarist, Tony Iommi, the central riff of "Heaven and Hell" is, frankly, a bit plodding and doesn't lend itself to much in the way of air guitar beyond, well, just standing there. There's some tasty soloing in the second half of this Ronnie James Dio–fronted epic, but you and any audience will be nodding off long before then.

"ONCE I DISCOVERED ITUNES, I GOT SO EXCITED, I SPENT THE NIGHT FINDING ALBUMS THAT I HAD HAD THAT I JUST COULDN'T FIND ANY MORE: *NOT SO QUIET ON THE WESTERN FRONT*, THE ALTERNATIVE TENTACLES COMPILATION FROM THE '80S, SABBATH'S *HEAVEN AND HELL*, ABBA'S *GREATEST HITS*. . ."—DAVE GROHL

Try this instead: "Symptom of the Universe" (*Sabotage*, 1975)

Iommi: A bit plodding

"Every Rose Has Its Thorn"

POISON

Open Up and Say . . . Ahh!, 1988

It smoothed Bill and Ted's entry into heaven, but this wistful power ballad will smooth nothing but your exit from any self-respecting rock club. "'Every Rose . . .' completely killed the metal in the pop metal scene, man," complained Dee Snider of Twisted Sister. "All of a sudden, all the heavy metal rock bands got rid of their distortion pedals and went acoustic."

"[GUITARIST] C.C. [DEVILLE] HAS ALWAYS BEEN THE METAL, RAWK ONE IN THE GROUP, AND HE THOUGHT I WAS A FUCKING SELL-OUT. HE HATED PLAYING 'EVERY ROSE . . .' THE SONG IS ONE OF THE REASONS HE REFUSES TO SPEAK TO ME ANYMORE. ALTHOUGH I THINK ME SLEEPING WITH HIS GIRLFRIEND OF SIX YEARS DIDN'T HELP EITHER."—BRET MICHAELS

Try this instead: "Talk Dirty to Me" (*Look What the Cat Dragged In*, 1986)

"Closer"

NINE INCH NAILS

The Downward Spiral, 1994

Oddly enough for a modern rock classic, the guitar is a mere fleeting background element on "Closer." Observed Tommy Lee of Mötley Crüe: "You can fuck to it, you can dance to it, and you can break shit to it." You cannot, however, air guitar to it.

"MUSICALLY, I THOUGHT IT WAS RIDICULOUS, IN ITS DISCO OVERTONES AND BLUNTNESS."—TRENT REZNOR

Try this instead: "Getting Smaller" (*With Teeth*, 2005)

"Kashmir"

LED ZEPPELIN

Physical Graffiti, 1975

Short of recruiting John Paul Jones (not too hard, given that he once produced the Butthole Surfers) and resurrecting John Bonham (a bit trickier) to back you up, you will never, ever pull this off. Even Robert Plant and Jimmy Page needed over thirty musicians when they climaxed their *UnLedded* MTV show with it in 1994.

"IT POSSESSED ALL THE LATENT ENERGY AND POWER THAT WASN'T HEAVY METAL. IT WAS SOMETHING ELSE. IT WAS THE PRIDE OF LED ZEPPELIN."—ROBERT PLANT

Try this instead: "Whole Lotta Love" (*Led Zeppelin II*, 1969)

"Flight of Icarus"

IRON MAIDEN

Piece of Mind, 1983

Penned by guitarist Adrian Smith and frontman Bruce Dickinson, this was the first lead single from a Maiden album not to feature a writing credit for founder Steve Harris. This sop to band democracy resulted in the most dreadful song of their opening decade. Despite its transatlantic success at the time, the song was omitted from two of the band's hits compilations, and hasn't been performed live in over a quarter of a century. So why should *you* play it?

"WE TEND TO PLAY IT A LITTLE BIT FASTER LIVE. LOOKING BACK ON IT NOW, WE FEEL WE COULD HAVE PLAYED IT AT THE FASTER SPEED ON THE ALBUM."—STEVE HARRIS

Try this instead: Any other Iron Maiden song

Smith: Dreadful

AIR GUITAR CHAMPIONSHIPS

"WARS WOULD END AND ALL BAD THINGS WOULD GO AWAY IF EVERYONE JUST PLAYED AIR GUITAR."

This is the mantra of the international air guitar community, which has congregated in an official capacity every year since an inaugural world championship event in Finland in 1996.

There are, of course, no winners or losers in air guitar. The joy is in the playing. Nonetheless, the competitions—which occur around the globe from Belgium to Brazil—have done much to legitimize this once stigmatized activity. They even inspired the well-received 2006 documentary movie *Air Guitar Nation* by Alexandra Lipsitz (later the coproducer of Justin Beiber's *Never Say Never*).

Pete: Powerful

Eddie: Energetic

Billie Joe: Bouncy

Key to the events' appeal is that they celebrate, rather than mock, their inherent stupidity (not unlike a Kiss show). Lest anyone fear that the contestants take themselves too seriously, cast an eye over the pseudonyms that have been used: Rockness Monster, Air Lingus, Satan Whoppercock, Eddie Van Safeway, and our personal favorite, Geoff Leopard. Don't let an inability to come up with a punning moniker put you off, though—entertainingly prosaic entrants have called themselves things like The Shred and gotten away with it.

Proving that air guitar can bring people together, the events have seen groups compete—such as Piss (yes, you guessed it, a Kiss tribute—of sorts) and the self-explanatory Triple Slash. The latter, in fact, led what was claimed to be a world record-breaking attempt at the biggest ever air ensemble—over four thousand people at the UK's GuilFest in 2005 (headlined, appropriately enough, by Status Quo)—playing "Sweet Child o' Mine."

There is little emphasis on technical accuracy. As one entrant, *New York Times* writer Dan Crane, advised, "Don't focus on your fingering too much as you play. Remember, if you hit a bad note only you will know. Instead, engage the crowd: make eye contact, perch yourself on the monitor and flutter your tongue; make fans get out their air lighters."

Although it's still, inevitably, a male-dominated pastime, there have been two notable female victors: 2004's world air guitar cochampion MiRi "Sonyk-Rok" Park (whose performance of "Hot for Teacher" by Van Halen won her an amplifier designed, donated, and autographed by Brian May) and 2010's UK air guitar champion Sophie "Eddie Six Strings" Scutt (who won the final playoff against the gold lamé–clad Juan Nightstand, on The Darkness's "I Believe in a Thing Called Love," by high kicking and, we would venture, appealing more to the crowd's spirit, both hetero-sexual and sisterly).

Ultimately, however, it doesn't matter whether you air guitar competitively for an audience or for fun in the privacy of your own home. It doesn't matter whether you're in your business suit or your birthday suit (be advised that the latter choice, although always popular at air guitar championships, has never actually secured anyone the top prize). It doesn't matter if you switch merrily from guitar to bass to drums (a mandatory activity at Rush shows). No—as Angus Young once sagely intoned, "Don't think of technique or anything—just play!"

Gene: Mean

Pete: Ever present

Angus: Acrobatic

DEDICATION

This book is dedicated to Douglass and Sonia
MacDonald, whose playing of *Big Hits (High Tide and
Green Grass)*, *Dark Side of the Moon*, *Revolver* and
Buddy Holly's 20 Golden Greats made it inevitable
that I would one day be writing about air guitar.

ABOUT THE AUTHOR

Bruno MacDonald (www.brunomacdonald.com) wrote
Omnibus' *Rock Connections*, and coedited Cassell's *1001
Songs You Must Hear Before You Die* and *1001 Albums You
Must Hear Before You Die*. He has contributed to books
including Guinness' *British Hit Singles* and *Rockopedia*,
and *Rock: The Rough Guide*. His *Pink Floyd Through the
Eyes Of . . .*, published in 1997, is still in print in the United
States. Bruno has advocated amnesty for air guitarists
since being taken to see Kiss at the age of eleven.

USEFUL WEB ADDRESSES

See the excellent www.guitarworld.com and
www.performingsongwriter.com for further
six-string splendor and musical musings.